4/98

POETRY IN MOTION

POETRY IN MOTION

100 Poems from the Subways and Buses

Edited by

Molly Peacock
Elise Paschen
Neil Neches

W. W. Norton & Company / New York / London

First Edition

The text of this book is composed in 12/14.5 Fournier,
with the display set in Fournier and Helvetica.
Composition by Crane Typesetting Service, Inc.
Manufacturing by The Courier Companies, Inc.
Book design by Chris Welch.

Library of Congress Cataloging-in-Publication Data

Poetry in motion: 100 poems from the subways and buses / edited by Molly Peacock,
Elise Paschen, Neil Neches.
p.   cm.
Includes bibliographical references and index.
ISBN 0-393-03977-3.—ISBN 0-393-31458-8 (pbk.)
1. Poetry—Collections.   I. Peacock, Molly, date.
II. Paschen, Elise.   III. Neches, Neil.
PN6101.P542   1996

808.81—dc20   95-47922
CIP

W. W. Norton & Company, Inc., 500 Fifth Avenue,
New York, NY 10110   http://web.wwnorton.com
W. W. Norton & Company Ltd., 10 Coptic Street, London WC1A 1PU

1 2 3 4 5 6 7 8 9 0

This book, a collaboration between 🚇 New York City Transit and the Poetry Society of America 🎵, is dedicated to public-transportation riders and readers everywhere.

Contents

Introduction

"It spoke to me," a harried commuter says. He wants to know where he can buy a Poetry in Motion placard of "The Armful," a Robert Frost poem he has seen on the subway. A three year old won't stop talking about "Magic Words," an Inuit poem her mother read to her while they rode the bus. And a woman who commutes daily from Brooklyn into Manhattan tells us she watches for the selections as they change each month.

Once marginalized, poetry has become a surprising cultural feast that invites everyone to attend, and the Poetry in Motion program has provided a banquet for millions. People of all ages, from teenagers to grandparents, respond to language that—in its depth, truth, and feeling—gives them something to think about on the ride home.

Six months after the initial launch of four poems by Emily Dickinson, Lucille Clifton, W. B. Yeats, and Walt Whitman in October of 1992, our schedule of two different poems per month began in 4,000 subway cars and in 3,700 buses. In the fall of 1994, Crosswalks TV, an educational television network, began to air poetry spots developed from the Poetry in Motion selections, further extending the program's reach. Now the program is spreading across North American cities. Poetry in Motion in Chicago is on the way. Programs in Boston, Los Angeles, and Washington, D.C., are being proposed. There's interest in St. Louis and Toronto. In New York alone the poetry posters reach 5 million people daily—that's over 1 billion passengers each year.

Soon after the Poetry in Motion posters appeared, teachers began to use them in their classrooms. Then tourists and native New Yorkers began to buy the placards from the New York Transit Museum Gift Shop in Grand Central Terminal. One day a minister called for permission to put a Poetry in Motion selection into a sermon. And nuns asked for placards for their work with senior citizens. Inquiries have come from as far away as Argentina, Germany, and Ireland.

The poems are selected in collaboration with poets, lovers of poetry, and transit officials. We three editors meet in the Poetry Society office, underneath the portraits of poets who have influenced American letters since the organization began in 1910. We do extensive homework, looking for short poems that represent the varied voices of poets from the ancients right up to the present. Since nationalities representing the entire world ride on New York City's public transit, we try to reflect that world. We look for poems that will speak to all ethnicities, genders, ages. We look for voices that will stimulate the exhausted, inspire the frustrated, comfort the burdened, and enchant even the youngest passengers. Careful readers will notice that no poet is represented twice—except Edna St. Vincent Millay. It was impossible to check our enthusiasm for Millay.

Although we aim to select complete poems, a number are excerpted. (In the contents of this book, the titles of excerpts are preceded by the word *from*.) When we have made our choices, final approvals are given, and New York City Transit takes on the job of producing and distributing the poems.

This book represents one hundred of our selections that have been or will be featured on the Poetry in Motion placards. We dedicate it to all the reader-riders who love the poems on their routes. Now you have them for your own.

—Molly Peacock
Poetry Society of America
President 1989–1994

Preface

Good ideas rarely have a single author. Therefore, it was no surprise to me, when I returned from London in 1991, enthusiastic after seeing poems displayed in the London Underground, to learn that placing poetry in MTA New York City Transit subway cars and buses was in the minds of several people in our organization and the Poetry Society of America.

In the hurly-burly of urban life, nowhere more concentrated than in the New York City subway and buses, it is an extraordinary experience to lift your eyes and, for a few moments, be captured by some lines of poetry. They evoke a range of emotions—from perplexity to sadness to joy—and, in so doing, enrich the lives of all who partake.

Poetry in Motion, initiated in October 1992, can truly be said to have been an instant success. It has brought both the Poetry Society and MTA New York City Transit much favorable publicity and response. We are now jointly involved in contacting other transit systems in the United States and Canada to urge them to participate.

Special thanks must go to Molly Peacock, who as President of the Poetry

Society of America nurtured the program lovingly during its formative years; to Elise Paschen, Executive Director of the Poetry Society, whose enthusiasm knows no bounds; to Jack Lusk, Senior Vice President of MTA New York City Transit, who guided the program; and to Neil Neches of New York City Transit, who oversees the day-to-day management of the program. There are many others whose support has been valuable and much appreciated.

To quote Matthew Arnold, English poet and critic: "Poetry is simply the most beautiful, impressive and wisely effective mode of saying things, and hence its importance."

It's also fun to read.

—Alan F. Kiepper
President (1990–1996)
MTA New York City Transit

POETRY IN MOTION

Let there be new flowering

let there be new flowering
in the fields let the fields
turn mellow for the men
let the men keep tender
through the time let the time
be wrested from the war
let the war be won
let love be
at the end

Lucille Clifton (b. 1936)

from *Crossing Brooklyn Ferry*

Flood-tide below me! I see you face to face!
Clouds of the west—sun there half an hour high—I see you also face
    to face.
Crowds of men and women attired in the usual costumes, how curious
    you are to me!
On the ferry boats, the hundreds and hundreds that cross, returning
    home, are more curious to me than you suppose,
And you that shall cross from shore to shore years hence are more to
    me, and more in my meditations, than you might suppose.

Walt Whitman (1819–1892)

"Hope" is the thing with feathers

"Hope" is the thing with feathers—
That perches in the soul—
And sings the tune without the words—
And never stops—at all—

And sweetest—in the Gale is heard—
And sore must be the storm—
That could abash the little Bird
That kept so many warm—

I've heard it in the chillest land
And on the strangest Sea—
Yet, never, in Extremity,
It asked a crumb—of Me.

Emily Dickinson (1830–1886)

When You Are Old

When you are old and grey and full of sleep,
And nodding by the fire, take down this book,
And slowly read, and dream of the soft look
Your eyes had once, and of their shadows deep;

How many loved your moments of glad grace,
And loved your beauty with love false or true,
But one man loved the pilgrim soul in you,
And loved the sorrows of your changing face;

And bending down beside the glowing bars,
Murmur, a little sadly, how Love fled
And paced upon the mountains overhead
And hid his face amid a crowd of stars.

William Butler Yeats (1865–1939)

Hermandad

Homenaje a Claudio Ptolomeo

Soy hombre: duro poco
y es enorme la noche.
Pero miro hacia arriba:
las estrellas escriben.
Sin entender comprendo:
también soy escritura
y en este mismo instante
alguien me deletrea.

Octavio Paz (b. 1914)
Translated from the Spanish by Eliot Weinberger

Brotherhood

Homage to Claudius Ptolemy

I am a man: little do I last
and the night is enormous.
But I look up:
the stars write.
Unknowing I understand:
I too am written,
and at this very moment
someone spells me out.

Travel

The railroad track is miles away,
And the day is loud with voices speaking,
Yet there isn't a train goes by all day
But I hear its whistle shrieking.

All night there isn't a train goes by,
Though the night is still for sleep and dreaming,
But I see its cinders red on the sky,
And hear its engine steaming.

My heart is warm with the friends I make,
And better friends I'll not be knowing;
Yet there isn't a train I wouldn't take,
No matter where it's going.

Edna St. Vincent Millay (1892–1950)

Sir, You Are Tough

Sir, you are tough, and I am tough.
But who will write whose epitaph?

Joseph Brodsky (1940–1996)

Magic Words

after Nalungiaq

In the very earliest time,
when both people and animals lived on earth,
a person could become an animal if he wanted to
and an animal could become a human being.
Sometimes they were people
and sometimes animals
and there was no difference.
All spoke the same language.
That was the time when words were like magic.
The human mind had mysterious powers.
A word spoken by chance
might have strange consequences.
It would suddenly come alive
and what people wanted to happen could happen—
all you had to do was say it.

Nobody could explain this:
That's the way it was.

Translated from the Inuit by Edward Field

from _The Inferno, Canto I_

In the middle of the journey of our life
I found myself astray in a dark wood
where the straight road had been lost sight of.

Dante Alighieri (1265–1321)
Translated from the Italian by Seamus Heaney

from *What Are Years?*

    What is our innocence,
what is our guilt? All are
    naked, none is safe. And whence
is courage: the unanswered question,
the resolute doubt,—
dumbly calling, deafly listening—that
in misfortune, even death,
       encourages others
       and in its defeat, stirs

    the soul to be strong?

Marianne Moore (1887–1972)

from _The Love Song of J. Alfred Prufrock_

Let us go then, you and I,
When the evening is spread out against the sky
Like a patient etherised upon a table;
Let us go, through certain half-deserted streets,
The muttering retreats
Of restless nights in one-night cheap hotels
And sawdust restaurants with oyster-shells:
Streets that follow like a tedious argument
Of insidious intent
To lead you to an overwhelming question . . .
Oh, do not ask, "What is it?"
Let us go and make our visit.

T. S. Eliot (1888–1965)

Speech to the Young
Speech to the Progress-Toward
(Among Them Nora and Henry III)

Say to them,
say to the down-keepers,
the sun-slappers,
the self-soilers,
the harmony-hushers,
"Even if you are not ready for day
it cannot always be night."
You will be right.
For that is the hard home-run.
Live not for battles won.
Live not for the-end-of-the-song.
Live in the along.

Gwendolyn Brooks (b. 1917)

If There Is a Scheme

If there is a scheme,
perhaps this too is in the scheme,
as when a subway car turns on a switch,
the wheels screeching against the rails,
and the lights go out—
but are on again in a moment.

Charles Reznikoff (1894–1976)

The Armful

For every parcel I stoop down to seize
I lose some other off my arms and knees,
And the whole pile is slipping, bottles, buns—
Extremes too hard to comprehend at once,
Yet nothing I should care to leave behind.
With all I have to hold with, hand and mind
And heart, if need be, I will do my best
To keep their building balanced at my breast.
I crouch down to prevent them as they fall;
Then sit down in the middle of them all.
I had to drop the armful in the road.
And try to stack them in a better load.

Robert Frost (1874–1963)

from *To Autumn*

Season of mists and mellow fruitfulness,
   Close bosom-friend of the maturing sun:
Conspiring with him how to load and bless
   With fruit the vines that round the thatch-eaves run;
To bend with apples the mossed cottage-trees,
   And fill all fruit with ripeness to the core;
     To swell the gourd, and plump the hazel shells
With a sweet kernel; to set budding more,
   And still more, later flowers for the bees,
Until they think warm days will never cease,
      For Summer has o'er-brimmed their clammy cells.

John Keats (1795–1821)

Blackberry Eating

I love to go out in late September
among the fat, overripe, icy, black blackberries
to eat blackberries for breakfast,
the stalks very prickly, a penalty
they earn for knowing the black art
of blackberry-making; and as I stand among them
lifting the stalks to my mouth, the ripest berries
fall almost unbidden to my tongue,
as words sometimes do, certain peculiar words
like *strengths* or *squinched*,
many-lettered, one-syllabled lumps,
which I squeeze, squinch open, and splurge well
in the silent, startled, icy, black language
of blackberry-eating in late September.

Galway Kinnell (b. 1927)

To a Poor Old Woman

munching a plum on
the street a paper bag
of them in her hand

They taste good to her
They taste good
to her. They taste
good to her

You can see it by
the way she gives herself
to the one half
sucked out in her hand

Comforted
a solace of ripe plums
seeming to fill the air
They taste good to her

William Carlos Williams (1883–1963)

Delta

If you have taken this rubble for my past
raking through it for fragments you could sell
know that I long ago moved on
deeper into the heart of the matter

If you think you can grasp me, think again:
my story flows in more than one direction
a delta springing from the riverbed
with its five fingers spread

Adrienne Rich (b. 1929)

Variación	**Variations**

El remanso de aire
bajo la rama del eco.

El remanso del agua
bajo fronda de luceros.

El remanso de tu boca
bajo espesura de besos.

Federico García Lorca (1899–1936)
Translated from the Spanish by Lysander Kemp

The still waters of the air
under the bough of the echo.

The still waters of the water
under a frond of stars.

The still waters of your mouth
under a thicket of kisses.

Please Give This Seat to an Elderly or Disabled Person

I stood during the entire journey:
nobody offered me a seat
although I was at least a hundred years older than anyone else on board,
although the signs of at least three major afflictions
were visible on me:
Pride, Loneliness, and Art.

Nina Cassian (b. 1924)
Translated from the Romanian by Naomi Lazard

from _The Love Poems of Marichiko_

You ask me what I thought about
Before we were lovers.
The answer is easy.
Before I met you
I didn't have anything to think about.

Kenneth Rexroth (1905–1982)

from *The Mind Is an Ancient and Famous Capital*

The mind is a city like London,
Smoky and populous: it is a capital
Like Rome, ruined and eternal,
Marked by the monuments which no one
Now remembers. For the mind, like Rome, contains
Catacombs, aqueducts, amphitheatres, palaces,
Churches and equestrian statues, fallen, broken or soiled.
The mind possesses and is possessed by all the ruins
Of every haunted, hunted generation's celebration.

Delmore Schwartz (1913–1966)

Luck

Sometimes a crumb falls
From the tables of joy,
Sometimes a bone
Is flung.

To some people
Love is given,
To others
Only heaven.

Langston Hughes (1902–1967)

Let No Charitable Hope

Now let no charitable hope
Confuse my mind with images
Of eagle and of antelope:
I am in nature none of these.

I was, being human, born alone;
I am, being woman, hard beset;
I live by squeezing from a stone
The little nourishment I get.

In masks outrageous and austere
The years go by in single file;
But none has merited my fear,
And none has quite escaped my smile.

Elinor Wylie (1885–1928)

from *Coal*

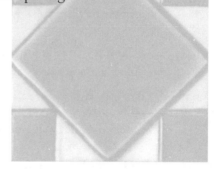

Love is a word, another kind of open.
As the diamond comes into a knot of flame
I am Black because I come from the earth's inside
now take my word for jewel in the open light.

Audre Lorde (1934–1992)

To My Love, Combing Her Hair

To my love, combing her hair
without a mirror, facing me,

a psalm: you've shampooed your hair, an entire
forest of pine trees is filled with yearning on your head.

Calmness inside and calmness outside
have hammered your face between them to a tranquil copper.

The pillow on your bed is your spare brain,
tucked under your neck for remembering and dreaming.

The earth is trembling beneath us, love.
Let's lie fastened together, a double safety-lock.

Yehuda Amichai (b. 1924)
Translated from the Hebrew by Chana Bloch and Stephen Mitchell

Mother of the Groom

What she remembers
Is his glistening back
In the bath, his small boots
In the ring of boots at her feet.

Hands in her voided lap,
She hears a daughter welcomed.
It's as if he kicked when lifted
And slipped her soapy hold.

Once soap would ease off
The wedding ring
That's bedded forever now
In her clapping hand.

Seamus Heaney (b. 1939)

from *Riding the A*

Wheels
and rails
in their prime
collide,
make love in a glide
of slickness
and friction.
It is an elation
I wish to pro-
long.
The station
is reached
too soon.

May Swenson (1919–1989)

Encounter

We were riding through frozen fields in a wagon at dawn.
A red wing rose in the darkness.

And suddenly a hare ran across the road.
One of us pointed to it with his hand.

That was long ago. Today neither of them is alive,
Not the hare, nor the man who made the gesture.

O my love, where are they, where are they going
The flash of a hand, streak of movement, rustle of pebbles.
I ask not out of sorrow, but in wonder.

Wilno, 1936
Czeslaw Milosz (b. 1911)
Translated from the Polish by Czeslaw Milosz and Lillian Vallee

from *I Am Vertical*

But I would rather be horizontal.
I am not a tree with my root in the soil
Sucking up minerals and motherly love
So that each March I may gleam into leaf,
Nor am I the beauty of a garden bed
Attracting my share of Ahs and spectacularly painted,
Unknowing I must soon unpetal.
Compared with me, a tree is immortal
And a flower-head not tall, but more startling,
And I want the one's longevity and the other's daring.

Sylvia Plath (1932–1963)

Western Wind

Western wind when wilt thou blow
the small rain down can rain
Christ if my love were in my arms
and I in my bed again

Anonymous (early sixteenth century)

Adolescence—I

In water-heavy nights behind grandmother's porch
We knelt in the tickling grass and whispered:
Linda's face hung before us, pale as a pecan,
And it grew wise as she said:
"A boy's lips are soft,
As soft as baby's skin."
The air closed over her words
A firefly whirred in the air, and in the distance
I could hear streetlamps ping
Into miniature suns
Against a feathery sky.

Rita Dove (b. 1952)

from *Antigone*
(lines 879–886)

Chorus:

Love, never conquered in battle
Love the plunderer laying waste the rich!
Love standing the night-watch
    guarding a girl's soft cheek,
you range the seas, the shepherds' steadings off in the wilds—
not even the deathless gods can flee your onset,
nothing human born for a day—
whoever feels your grip is driven mad.

Sophocles (496?–406 B.C.)
Translated from the Greek by Robert Fagles

Casabianca

Love's the boy stood on the burning deck
trying to recite "The boy stood on
the burning deck." Love's the son
 stood stammering elocution
 while the poor ship in flames went down.

Love's the obstinate boy, the ship,
even the swimming sailors, who
would like a schoolroom platform, too,
 or an excuse to stay
 on deck. And love's the burning boy.

Elizabeth Bishop (1911–1979)

A Man Said to the Universe

A man said to the universe:
"Sir, I exist!"
"However," replied the universe,
"The fact has not created in me
A sense of obligation."

Stephen Crane (1871–1900)

Summer

I like hot days, hot days
Sweat is what you got days
Bugs buzzin from cousin to cousin
Juices dripping
Running and ripping
Catch the one you love days

Birds peeping
Old men sleeping
Lazy days, daisies lay
Beaming and dreaming
Of hot days, hot days,
Sweat is what you got days

Walter Dean Myers (b. 1937)

from _Recuerdo_

We were very tired, we were very merry—
We had gone back and forth all night on the ferry;
And you ate an apple, and I ate a pear,
From a dozen of each we had bought somewhere;
And the sky went wan, and the wind came cold,
And the sun rose dripping, a bucketful of gold.

Edna St. Vincent Millay (1892–1950)

from *The Passionate Man's Pilgrimage*

Give me my scallop-shell of quiet,
My staff of faith to walk upon,
My scrip of joy, immortal diet,
My bottle of salvation,
My gown of glory, hope's true gage,
And thus I'll take my pilgrimage.

Sir Walter Ralegh (1552–1618)

Komu to yū mo　　　　　　**You Say, "I Will Come"**

Komu to yū mo　　　　　　You say, "I will come."
Konu toki aru wo　　　　　And you do not come.
Koji to yū wo　　　　　　Now you say, "I will not come."
Komu to wa mataji　　　　So I shall expect you.
Koji to yū mono wo　　　Have I learned to understand you?

Lady Ōtomo No Sakanoe (eighth century)
Translated from the Japanese by Kenneth Rexroth

from *Riding on a Railroad Train*

Oh, some like trips in luxury ships,
And some in gasoline wagons,
And others swear by the upper air
And the wings of flying dragons.
Let each make haste to indulge his taste,
Be it beer, champagne or cider;
My private joy, both man and boy,
Is being a railroad rider.

Ogden Nash (1902–1971)

love is a place

love is a place
& through this place of
love move
(with brightness of peace)
all places

yes is a world
& is in this world of
yes live
(skilfully curled)
all worlds

E. E. Cummings (1894–1962)

Unfortunate Coincidence

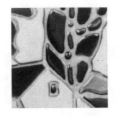

By the time you swear you're his,
   Shivering and sighing,
And he vows his passion is
   Infinite, undying—
Lady, make a note of this:
   One of you is lying.

Dorothy Parker (1893–1967)

from 'Back on Times Square, Dreaming of Times Square'

Let some sad trumpeter stand
      on the empty streets at dawn
and blow a silver chorus to the
      buildings of Times Square,
memorial of ten years, at 5 A.M., with
      the thin white moon just
          visible
      above the green & grooking McGraw
      Hill Offices
a cop walks by, but he's invisible
      with his music

New York, July 1958
Allen Ginsberg (b. 1926)

For Friendship

For friendship
make a chain that holds,
to be bound to
others, two by two,

a walk, a garland,
handed by hands
that cannot move
unless they hold.

Robert Creeley (b. 1926)

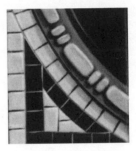

Aspects of Eve

To have been one
of many ribs
and to be chosen.
To grow into something
quite different
knocking finally
as a bone knocks
on the closed gates of the garden—
which unexpectedly
open.

Linda Pastan (b. 1932)

Sandinista Avioncitos

The little airplanes of the heart
with their brave little propellers
What can they do
against the winds of darkness
even as butterflies are beaten back
by hurricanes
yet do not die
They lie in wait wherever
they can hide and hang
their fine wings folded
and when the killer-wind dies
they flutter forth again
into the new-blown light
live as leaves

Lawrence Ferlinghetti (b. 1919)

Thank You, My Dear

Thank you, my dear

You came, and you did
well to come: I needed
you. You have made

love blaze up in
my breast—bless you!
Bless you as often

as the hours have
been endless to me
while you were gone.

Sappho (c. 600 B.C.)
Translated from the Greek by Mary Barnard

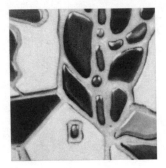

Transit

A woman I have never seen before
Steps from the darkness of her town-house door
At just that crux of time when she is made
So beautiful that she or time must fade.

What use to claim that as she tugs her gloves
A phantom heraldry of all the loves
Blares from the lintel? That the staggered sun
Forgets, in his confusion, how to run?

Still, nothing changes as her perfect feet
Click down the walk that issues in the street,
Leaving the stations of her body there
As a whip maps the countries of the air.

Richard Wilbur (b. 1921)

I Stop Writing the Poem

to fold the clothes. No matter who lives
or who dies, I'm still a woman.
I'll always have plenty to do.
I bring the arms of his shirt
together. Nothing can stop
our tenderness. I'll get back
to the poem. I'll get back to being
a woman. But for now
there's a shirt, a giant shirt
in my hands, and somewhere a small girl
standing next to her mother
watching to see how it's done.

Tess Gallagher (b. 1943)

from *Thirteen Ways of Looking at a Blackbird*

Among twenty snowy mountains,
The only moving thing
Was the eye of the blackbird.

The blackbird whirled in the autumn winds.
It was a small part of the pantomime.

I do not know which to prefer,
The beauty of inflections
Or the beauty of innuendoes,
The blackbird whistling
Or just after.

Wallace Stevens (1879–1955)

First Memory

Long ago, I was wounded. I lived
to revenge myself
against my father, not
for what he was—
for what I was: from the beginning of time,
in childhood, I thought
that pain meant
I was not loved.
It meant I loved.

Louise Glück (b. 1943)

Hedgehog

He ambles along like a walking pin cushion,
Stops and curls up like a chestnut burr.
He's not worried because he's so little.
Nobody is going to slap him around.

Chu Chen Po (ninth century)
Translated from the Chinese by Kenneth Rexroth

Suspended

I had grasped God's garment in the void
but my hand slipped
on the rich silk of it.
The 'everlasting arms' my sister loved to remember
must have upheld my leaden weight
from falling, even so,
for though I claw at empty air and feel
nothing, no embrace,
I have not plummetted.

Denise Levertov (b. 1923)

Listen to the Mustn'ts

Listen to the MUSTN'TS, child,
Listen to the DON'TS
Listen to the SHOULDN'TS
The IMPOSSIBLES, the WON'TS
Listen to the NEVER HAVES
Then listen close to me—
Anything can happen, child,
ANYTHING can be.

Shel Silverstein

The Question

People always say to me
"What do you think you'd like to be
When you grow up?"
And I say "Why,
I think I'd like to be the sky
Or be a plane or train or mouse
Or maybe a haunted house
Or something furry, rough and wild . . .
Or maybe I will stay a child."

Karla Kuskin (b. 1932)

The Bagel

I stopped to pick up the bagel
rolling away in the wind,
annoyed with myself
for having dropped it
as it were a portent.
Faster and faster it rolled,
with me running after it
bent low, gritting my teeth,
and I found myself doubled over
and rolling down the street
head over heels, one complete somersault
after another like a bagel
and strangely happy with myself.

David Ignatow (b. 1914)

Reflective

I found a
weed
that had a

mirror in it
and that
mirror

looked in at
a mirror
in

me that
had a
weed in it

A. R. Ammons (b. 1926)

My Heart Leaps Up

My heart leaps up when I behold
   A rainbow in the sky:
So was it when my life began;
So is it now I am a man;
So be it when I shall grow old,
   Or let me die!
The Child is father of the Man;
And I could wish my days to be
Bound each to each by natural piety.

William Wordsworth (1770–1850)

Heat

O wind, rend open the heat,
cut apart the heat,
rend it to tatters.

Fruit cannot drop
through this thick air—
fruit cannot fall into heat
that presses up and blunts
the points of pears
and rounds the grapes.

Cut the heat—
plough through it,
turning it on either side
of your path.

H.D. (Hilda Doolittle, 1886–1961)

from *Ode to the Cat*

There was something wrong
with the animals:
their tails were too long, and they had
unfortunate heads.
Then they started coming together,
little by little
fitting together to make a landscape,
developing birthmarks, grace, pep.
But the cat,
only the cat
turned out finished,
and proud:
born in a state of total completion,
it sticks to itself and knows exactly what it wants.

Pablo Neruda (1904–1973)
Translated from the Spanish by Ken Krabbenhoft

First Grade

In the play Amy didn't want to be
anybody; so she managed the curtain.
Sharon wanted to be Amy. But Sam
wouldn't let anybody be anybody else—
he said it was wrong. "All right," Steve said,
"I'll be me but I don't like it."
So Amy was Amy, and we didn't have the play.
And Sharon cried.

William Stafford (1914–1993)

from *Manhattan*

We'll have Manhattan,
The Bronx and Staten
Island too.
It's lovely going through
The zoo.
It's very fancy
On old Delancey
Street, you know.
The subway charms us so
When balmy breezes blow
To and fro.
And tell me what street
Compares with Mott Street
In July?
Sweet pushcarts gently gliding by.

The great big city's a wondrous toy
Just made for a girl and boy.
We'll turn Manhattan
Into an isle of joy.

Lorenz Hart (1895–1943)

The Talker

One person present steps on his pedal of speech
and, like a faulty drinking fountain, it spurts
all over the room in facts and puns and jokes,
on books, on people, on politics, on sports,

on everything. Two or three others, gathered
to chat, must bear his unending monologue
between their impatient heads like a giant buzz
of a giant fly, or magnanimous bullfrog

croaking for all the frogs in the world. Amid
the screech of traffic or in a hubbub crowd
he climbs the decibels toward some glorious view.
I think he only loves himself out loud.

Mona Van Duyn (b. 1921)

Jamesian

Their relationship consisted
In discussing if it existed.

Thom Gunn (b. 1929)

from *Grasmere*

for Lois Squires

Rainstorms that blacken like a headache
where mosses thicken, and the mornings
smell of jonquils, the stillness
of hung fells thronged with the primaveral
noise of waterfalls—contentment
pours in spate from every slope; the lake fills,
the kingcups drown, and still it rains,
the sheep graze, their black lambs bounce
and skitter in the wet: such weather
one cannot say, here, why
one is still so happy.

Amy Clampitt (1920–1994)

Revival

Snow is a mind
falling, a continuous breath
of climbs, loops, spirals,
dips into the earth
like white fireflies
wanting to land, finding
a wind between houses,
diving like moths
into their own light
so that one wonders
if snow is a wing's
long memory across winter.

Steve Crow (b. 1949)

from *Yes*

Some go local
Some go express
Some can't wait
To answer Yes.

Some complain
Of strain and stress
Their answer may be
No for Yes.

Some like failure
Some like success
Some like Yes Yes
Yes Yes Yes.

Open your eyes,
Dream but don't guess.
Your biggest surprise
Comes after Yes.

Muriel Rukeyser (1913–1979)

from *Do Not Go Gentle into That Good Night*

Do not go gentle into that good night,
Old age should burn and rave at close of day;
Rage, rage against the dying of the light.

Though wise men at their end know dark is right,
Because their words had forked no lightning they
Do not go gentle into that good night.

Dylan Thomas (1914–1953)

Precautions

Not incorrectly
they had advised me
to use the long spoon
if I went to dine with the devil.
Unfortunately
on those rare occasions
the only one available
was short.

Eugenio Montale (1896–1981)
Translated from the Italian by Jonathan Galassi

A Renewal

Having used every subterfuge
To shake you, lies, fatigue, or even that of passion,
Now I see no way but a clean break.
I add that I am willing to bear the guilt.

You nod assent. Autumn turns windy, huge,
A clear vase of dry leaves vibrating on and on.
We sit, watching. When I next speak
Love buries itself in me, up to the hilt.

James Merrill (1926–1995)

Those Winter Sundays

Sundays too my father got up early
and put his clothes on in the blueblack cold,
then with cracked hands that ached
from labor in the weekday weather made
banked fires blaze. No one ever thanked him.

I'd wake and hear the cold splintering, breaking.
When the rooms were warm, he'd call,
and slowly I would rise and dress,
fearing the chronic angers of that house,

Speaking indifferently to him,
who had driven out the cold
and polished my good shoes as well.
What did I know, what did I know
of love's austere and lonely offices?

Robert Hayden (1913–1980)

The Moon's the North Wind's Cooky
(What the little girl said)

The Moon's the North Wind's cooky.
He bites it, day by day,
Until there's but a rim of scraps,
That crumble all away.

The South Wind is a baker.
He kneads clouds in his den,
And bakes a crisp new moon *that . . . greedy*
North . . . Wind . . . eats . . . again!

Vachel Lindsay (1879–1931)

An Obsessive Combination of
Ontological Inscape, Trickery and Love

Busy, with an idea for a code, I write
signals hurrying from left to right,
or right to left, by obscure routes,
for my own reasons; taking a word like "writes"
down tiers of tries until its secret rites
make sense; or until, suddenly, RATS
can amazingly and funnily become STAR
and right to left that small star
is mine, for my own liking, to stare
its five lucky pins inside out, to store
forever kindly, as if it were a star
I touched and a miracle I really wrote.

Anne Sexton (1928–1974)

I Am Singing the Cold Rain

for Charles White Antelope

i am singing the cold rain
i am singing the winter dawn
i am turning in the gray morning
of my life
toward home

ni hoi nim mi ni hon   ido mi moo
ni hoi nim mi ni hon   e inif
ni hoi das i woi nu
na wodstan ni hi vist
na dutz   na ho utz

Lance Henson (b. 1944)
Translated from the Cheyenne by the author

The Panther

In the Jardin des Plantes, Paris

His vision, from the constantly passing bars,
has grown so weary that it cannot hold
anything else. It seems to him there are
a thousand bars; and behind the bars, no world.

As he paces in cramped circles, over and over,
the movement of his powerful soft strides
is like a ritual dance around a center
in which a mighty will stands paralyzed.

Only at times, the curtain of the pupils
lifts, quietly—. An image enters in,
rushes down through the tensed, arrested muscles,
plunges into the heart and is gone.

Rainer Maria Rilke (1875–1926)
Translated from the German by Stephen Mitchell

Cartography

As you lay in sleep
I saw the chart
Of artery and vein
Running from your heart,

Plain as the strength
Marked upon the leaf
Along the length,
Mortal and brief,

Of your gaunt hand.
I saw it clear:
The wiry brand
Of the life we bear

Mapped like the great
Rivers that rise
Beyond our fate
And distant from our eyes.

Louise Bogan (1897–1970)

Days

What are days for?
Days are where we live.
They come, they wake us
Time and time over.
They are to be happy in:
Where can we live but days?

Ah, solving that question
Brings the priests and the doctor
In their long coats
Running over the fields.

3 August 1953
Philip Larkin (1922–1985)

from *Lullaby*

Lay your sleeping head, my love,
Human on my faithless arm;
Time and fevers burn away
Individual beauty from
Thoughtful children, and the grave
Proves the child ephemeral:
But in my arms till break of day
Let the living creature lie,
Mortal, guilty, but to me
The entirely beautiful.

W. H. Auden (1907–1973)

Wall

Simple and extraordinary wall.
Wall without weight and without color:
a hint of air in the air.

From a hillside, birds pass,
light passes like a swing,
the edge of winter passes
like a breath of summer.
A leafy wind
and embodied shadows pass.

But a sigh does not break bounds,
arms do not meet,
and no heart-to-heart is made flesh.

Gabriela Mistral (1889–1957)
Translated from the Spanish by Maria Giachetti

As Much As You Can

And if you cannot make your life as you want it,
at least try this
as much as you can: do not disgrace it
in the crowding contact with the world,
in the many movements and all the talk.

Do not disgrace it by taking it,
dragging it around often and exposing it
to the daily folly
of relationships and associations,
till it becomes like an alien burdensome life.

C. P. Cavafy (1863–1933)
Translated from the Greek by Edmund Keeley
and Philip Sherrard

Birth

When they were wild
When they were not yet human
When they could have been anything,
I was on the other side ready with milk to lure them,
And their father, too, each name a net in his hands.

Louise Erdrich (b. 1954)

Take Hands

Take hands.
There is no love now.
But there are hands.
There is no joining now,
But a joining has been
of the fastening of fingers
And their opening.
More than the clasp even, the kiss
Speaks loneliness,
How we dwell apart
And how love triumphs in this.

Laura Riding Jackson (1901–1991)

from *The Round*

Light splashed this morning
on the shell-pink anemones
swaying on their tall stems;
down blue-spiked veronica
light flowed in rivulets
over the humps of the honeybees;
this morning I saw light kiss
the silk of the roses
in their second flowering,
my late bloomers
flushed with their brandy.
A curious gladness shook me . . .

I can scarcely wait till tomorrow
when a new life begins for me
as it does each day,
as it does each day.

Stanley Kunitz (b. 1905)

You Called Me Corazón

That was enough
for me to forgive you.
To spirit a tiger
from its cell.

Called me *corazón*
in that instant before
I let go the phone
back to its cradle.

Your voice small.
Heat of your eyes,
how I would've placed
my mouth on each.

Said *corazón*
and the word blazed
like a branch of *jacaranda*.

Sandra Cisneros (b. 1954)

My Heart

I'm not going to cry all the time
nor shall I laugh all the time,
I don't prefer one "strain" to another.
I'd have the immediacy of a bad movie,
not just a sleeper, but also the big,
overproduced first-run kind. I want to be
at least as alive as the vulgar. And if
some aficionado of my mess says "That's
not like Frank!", all to the good! I
don't wear brown and grey suits all the time,
do I? No. I wear workshirts to the opera,
often. I want my feet to be bare,
I want my face to be shaven, and my heart—
you can't plan on the heart, but
the better part of it, my poetry, is open.

Frank O'Hara (1926–1966)

Autumn Leaves

The dead piled up, thick, fragrant, on the fire escape.
My mother ordered me again, and again, to sweep it clean.
All that blooms must fall. I learned this not from the Tao,
   but from high school biology.

Oh, the contradictions of having a broom and not a dustpan!
I swept the leaves down, down through the iron grille
and let the dead rain over the Wong family's patio.

And it was Achilles Wong who completed the task.
   We called her:
The-one-who-cleared-away-another-family's-autumn.
She blossomed, tall, benevolent, notwithstanding.

Marilyn Chin (b. 1955)

Window

Night from a railroad car window
Is a great, dark, soft thing
Broken across with slashes of light.

Carl Sandburg (1878–1967)

The Sloth

In moving slow he has no Peer.
You ask him something in his Ear,
He thinks about it for a Year;

And, then, before he says a Word
There, upside down (unlike a Bird),
He will assume that you have Heard—

A most Ex-as-per-at-ing Lug.
But should you call his manner Smug,
He'll sigh and give his Branch a Hug;

Then off again to Sleep he goes,
Still swaying gently by his Toes,
And you just *know* he knows he knows.

Theodore Roethke (1908–1963)

Four in the Morning

The hour from night to day.
The hour from side to side.
The hour for those past thirty.

The hour swept clean to the crowing of cocks.
The hour when earth betrays us.
The hour when wind blows from extinguished stars.
The hour of and-what-if-nothing-remains-after-us.

The hollow hour.
Blank, empty.
The very pit of all other hours.

No one feels good at four in the morning.
If ants feel good at four in the morning
—three cheers for the ants. And let five o'clock come
if we're to go on living.

Wisława Szymborska (b. 1923)
Translated from the Polish by Magnus J. Krynski and Robert A. Maguire

DANS
FLETS   CE
RE   MI
LES   ROIR
SONT   JE
ME   SUIS
COM   EN
NON   Guillaume   CLOS
ET   Apollinaire   VI
GES   VANT
AN   ET
LES   VRAI
NE   COM
   GI   ME
     MA   ON
         I

IN THIS
IONS   MIR
FLECT   ROR
RE   I
THE   AM
LIKE   Guillaume   EN
NOT   Apollinaire   CLOSED
AND   A
GELS   LIVE
AN   AND
GINE   REAL
   MA   AS
     I   YOU

Guillaume Apollinaire (1880–1918)
Translated from the French by Kenneth Koch

Star

If, in the light of things, you fade
real, yet wanly withdrawn
to our determined and appropriate
distance, like the moon left on
all night among the leaves, may
you invisibly delight this house;
O star, doubly compassionate, who came
too soon for twilight, too late
for dawn, may your pale flame
direct the worst in us
through chaos
with the passion of
plain day.

Derek Walcott (b. 1930)

Happiness

A state you must dare not enter
   with hopes of staying,
quicksand in the marshes, and all

the roads leading to a castle
   that doesn't exist.
But there it is, as promised,

with its perfect bridge above
   the crocodiles,
and its doors forever open.

Stephen Dunn (b. 1939)

Winter Poem

once a snowflake fell
on my brow and i loved
it so much i kissed
it and it was happy and called its cousins
and brothers and a web
of snow engulfed me then
i reached to love them all
and i squeezed them and they became
a spring rain and i stood perfectly
still and was a flower

Nikki Giovanni (b. 1943)

from *Romeo and Juliet*

Act III, Scene ii

Come, night, come, Romeo, come, thou day in night,
For thou wilt lie upon the wings of night
Whiter than new snow on a raven's back.
Come, gentle night, come, loving, black-browed night,
Give me my Romeo, and, when he shall die,
Take him and cut him out in little stars,
And he will make the face of heaven so fine
That all the world will be in love with night,
And pay no worship to the garish sun.
Oh, I have bought the mansion of a love,
But not possessed it, and though I am sold,
Not yet enjoyed.

William Shakespeare (1566–1616)

Along the Hard Crest of the Snowdrift

Along the hard crest of the snowdrift
to my white, mysterious house,
both of us quiet now,
keeping silent as we walk.
And sweeter than any song
this dream we now complete—
the trembling of branches we brush against,
the soft ringing of your spurs.

Anna Akhmatova (1889–1966)
Translated from the Russian by Jane Kenyon

To My Dear and Loving Husband

If ever two were one, then surely we.
If ever man were loved by wife, then thee;
If ever wife was happy in a man,
Compare with me, ye women, if you can.
I prize thy love more than whole mines of gold
Or all the riches that the East doth hold.
My love is such that rivers cannot quench,
Nor ought but love from thee, give recompense.
Thy love is such I can no way repay,
The heavens reward thee manifold, I pray.
Then while we live, in love let's so persevere
That when we live no more, we may live ever.

Anne Bradstreet (1612–1672)

from *Marriage*

When she introduces me to her parents
back straightened, hair finally combed, strangled by a tie,
should I sit knees together on their 3rd degree sofa
and not ask Where's the bathroom?
How else to feel other than I am,
often thinking Flash Gordon soap—
O how terrible it must be for a young man
seated before a family and the family thinking
We never saw him before! He wants our Mary Lou!
After tea and homemade cookies they ask What do you do for a living?

Gregory Corso (b. 1930)

Song of Solomon 2:8–13

The voice of my beloved! behold, he cometh leaping
upon the mountains, skipping upon the hills.

My beloved is like a roe, or a young hart: behold,
he standeth behind our wall, he looketh forth at the
windows, shewing himself through the lattice.

My beloved spake, and said unto me,
Rise up, my love, my fair one, and come away.

For lo, the winter is past, the rain is over, and gone;

The flowers appear on the earth; the time of the singing of
birds is come, and the voice of the turtle is heard in our land.

The fig tree putteth forth her green figs,
and the vines with the tender grape give a good smell.
Arise, my love, my fair one, and come away.

The King James Bible (1611)

Two Haiku Poems

Don't worry, spiders,
I keep house
    casually.

    Mosquito at my ear—
Does it think
    I'm deaf?

Kobayashi Issa (1763–1827)
Translated from the Japanese by Robert Hass

from *Lost Sister*

In China,
even the peasants
named their first daughters
Jade—
the stone that in the far fields
could moisten the dry season,
could make men move mountains
for the healing green of the inner hills
glistening like slices of winter melon.

Cathy Song (b. 1955)

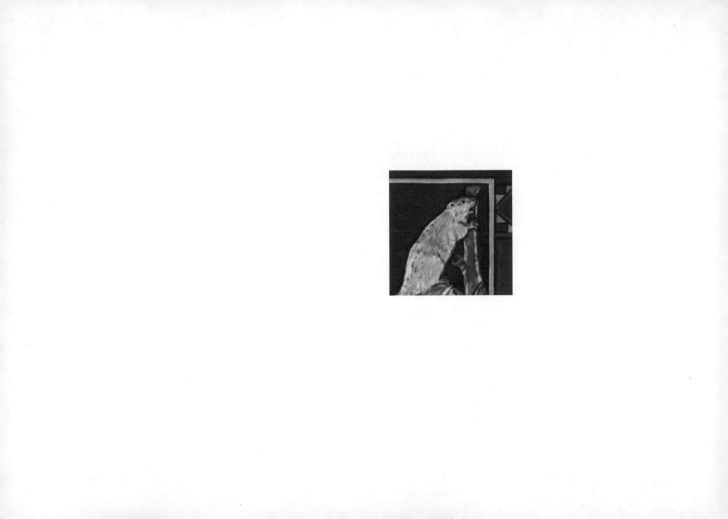

Selected Bibliography

Akhmatova, Anna. *Selected Poems*. Viking Penguin, New York, 1992. D. M. Thomas, trans. *From Room to Room*. alicejames books, Cambridge, Mass., 1978. Jane Kenyon, trans.

Amichai, Yehuda. *The Selected Poetry of Yehuda Amichai*. HarperCollins Publishers, Inc., New York, 1986. Chana Bloch and Stephen Mitchell, trans.

Ammons, A. R. *Selected Poems, Expanded Edition*. W. W. Norton & Company, Inc., New York, 1987. *Tape for the Turn of the Year*. W. W. Norton & Company, Inc., New York, 1994.

Apollinaire, Guillaume. *Alcools: Poems*. University Press of New England, Hanover, 1995. Donald Revell, trans. *Rose, Where Did You Get That Red?* Random House, New York, 1973. Kenneth Koch, trans.

Auden, W. H. *Collected Poems*. Vintage International Series, Random House, Inc., New York, 1991.

Bishop, Elizabeth. *The Complete Poems: 1927–1979*. Farrar, Straus & Giroux, New York, 1983.

Bogan, Louise. *The Blue Estuaries: Poems, 1923–1968*. The Ecco Press, Hopewell, N.J., 1977.

Bradstreet, Anne. *The Works of Anne Bradstreet*. The John Harvard Library Series, Belknap Press of Harvard University Press, Cambridge, 1990.

Brodsky, Joseph. *So Forth: Poems*. Farrar, Straus & Giroux, New York, 1995.

Brooks, Gwendolyn. *Blacks*. Third World Press, Chicago, 1991. *Selected Poems*. HarperCollins, Inc., New York, 1982.

Cassian, Nina. *Life Sentences*: *Selected Poems*. W. W. Norton & Company, Inc., New York, 1991. *Cheerleader for a Funeral*: *Poems*. Dufour Editions, Inc., Chester Springs, 1993.

Cavafy, C. P. *The Complete Poems of Cavafy*. Harcourt, Brace & Jovanovich, Orlando, 1976. Rae Dalven, trans. *C. P. Cavafy*: *Collected Poems*. Princeton University Press, Princeton, N.J., 1992. George Savidis, ed., Edmund Keeley and Philip Sherrard, trans.

Chin, Marilyn. *The Phoenix Gone, the Terrace Empty*: *Poems*. Milkweed Editions, Minneapolis, 1994.

Cisneros, Sandra. *Loose Woman*. Random House, Inc., New York, 1995.

Clampitt, Amy. *A Silence Opens*: *Poems*. Alfred A. Knopf, Inc., New York, 1994.

Clifton, Lucille. *Book of Light*. Copper Canyon Press, Port Townsend, Wash., 1993.

Corso, Gregory. *Mindfield*: *New & Selected Poems*. Thunder's Mouth Press, New York, 1989.

Creeley, Robert. *The Collected Poems of Robert Creeley, 1945–1975*. University of California Press, Berkeley, 1982.

Cummings, E. E. *Complete Poems 1904–1962*. Liveright Publishing Corp., New York, 1994.

Dante, Alighieri. *Dante's Inferno*: *Translations by Twenty Contemporary Poets*. The Ecco Press, Hopewell, N.J., 1994. Daniel Halpern, ed. *The Inferno of Dante*: *A New Verse Translation*. Farrar, Straus & Giroux, New York, 1994. Robert Pinsky, trans.

Dickinson, Emily. *The Complete Poems of Emily Dickinson*. Little, Brown and Company, New York, 1960. Thomas H. Johnson, ed.

Doolittle, Hilda. *Collected Poems, 1912–1944*. New Directions Publishing Corp., New York, 1986.

Dove, Rita. *Selected Poems of Rita Dove*. Random House, Inc., New York, 1993.

Dunn, Stephen. *New and Selected Poems, 1974–1994*. W. W. Norton & Company, Inc., New York, 1994.

Eliot, T. S. *The Complete Poems & Plays, 1909–1950*. Harcourt Brace & Co., San Diego, 1952.

Erdrich, Louise. *Baptism of Desire*: *Poems*. HarperCollins, Inc., New York, 1990.

Ferlinghetti, Lawrence. *These Are My Rivers*: *New & Selected Poems, 1955–1993*. New Directions Publishing Corp., New York, 1994.

Frost, Robert. *The Poetry of Robert Frost*. Henry Holt & Company, Inc., New York, 1979.

Gallagher, Tess. *Amplitude*: *New & Selected Poems*. Graywolf Press, Saint Paul, Minn., 1988.

García, Lorca Federico. *Selected Poems*. Farrar, Straus & Giroux, New York, 1994. Christopher Maurer, ed.

Ginsberg, Allen. *White Shroud*: *Poems 1980–1985*. Harper & Row, Inc., New York, 1986. *Cosmopolitan Greetings*: *Poems 1986–1992*. HarperCollins Publishers, Inc., 1994.

Giovanni, Nikki. *My House*. William Morrow & Co., Inc., New York, 1974.

Glück, Louise. *The First Four Books of Poems*. The Ecco Press, Hopewell, N.J., 1995. *Wild Iris: Poems*. The Ecco Press, Hopewell, N.J., 1993.

Gunn, Thom. *Collected Poems*. Farrar, Straus & Giroux, New York, 1995.

Hayden, Robert. *Collected Poems*. Liveright Publishing Corp., New York, 1996.

Heaney, Seamus. *Selected Poems 1966–1987*. Farrar, Straus & Giroux, New York, 1993. *Seeing Things: Poems*. Farrar, Straus & Giroux, New York, 1993.

Hughes, Langston. *Selected Poems of Langston Hughes*. Vintage Classics Series, Random House, Inc., New York, 1990.

Ignatow, David. *Against the Evidence*: *Selected Poems, 1934–1994*. University Press of New England, Hanover, 1994.

Issa, Kobayashi. *Issa*: *Cup-of-Tea Poems*: *Selected Haiku of Kobayashi Issa*. Jain Publishing Co., Fremont, 1994. David G. Lanoue, trans. *The Essential Haiku*: *Versions of Basho, Buson, and Issa*. The Ecco Press, Hopewell, N.J., 1994. Robert Hass, trans.

Jackson, Laura (Riding). "*The Poems of Laura Riding*: *A New Edition from the 1938 Collection*. Persea Books, New York, 1980.

Keats, John. *Poetical Works of John Keats*. Oxford Standard Authors Series, Oxford University Press, Inc., New York, 1961. Heathcote W. Garrod, ed. *The Essential Keats*. The Ecco Press, Hopewell, N.J., 1987. Philip Levine, ed.

Kinnell, Galway. *Selected Poems*. Houghton Mifflin Co., Boston, 1983. *Imperfect Thirst*. Houghton Mifflin Co., Boston, 1994.

Kunitz, Stanley. *Poems of Stanley Kunitz, Nineteen Twenty-Seven to Nineteen Seventy-Eight*. Little, Brown and Company, New York, 1979. *Passing Through*: *The Later Poems, New and Selected*. W. W. Norton & Company, Inc., New York, 1995.

Kuskin, Karla. *I Thought I'd Take My Rat to School*: *Poems for September to June*. Little, Brown and Company, New York, 1993. Abby Carter, illus.

Larkin, Philip. *Collected Poems*. Farrar, Straus & Giroux, New York, 1989. Anthony Thwaite, ed.

Levertov, Denise. *Tesserae*. New Directions Publishing Corp., New York, 1995.

Lindsay, Vachel. *Selected Poems of Vachel Lindsay*. Macmillan Publishing Co., Inc., New York, 1986.

Lorde, Audre. *Our Dead Behind Us*. W. W. Norton & Company, Inc., New York, 1994.

Merrill, James. *Selected Poems, 1946–1985*. Alfred A. Knopf, Inc., New York, 1992. *A Scattering of Salts*. Alfred A. Knopf, Inc., New York, 1995.

Millay, Edna St. Vincent. *Collected Poems*. HarperCollins Publishers, Inc., New York, 1981. Norma Millay, ed.

Milosz, Czeslaw. *Collected Poems*. The Ecco Press, Hopewell, N.J., 1980.

Montale, Eugenio. *Cuttlefish Bones*. W. W. Norton & Company, Inc., New York, 1993. William

Arrowsmith, trans. *Otherwise: Last and First Poems of Eugenio Montale.* Random House, New York, 1984. Jonathan Galassi, trans.

Moore, Marianne. *Complete Poems.* Viking Penguin, New York, 1994.

Myers, Walter Dean. *Brown Angels: An Album of Pictures & Verse.* HarperCollins Children's Books, New York, 1993.

Nash, Ogden. *I'm a Stranger Here Myself.* Buccaneer Books, Inc., Cutchogee, 1994.

Neruda, Pablo. *Five Decades: Poems 1925–1970.* Grove Atlantic, Inc., New York, 1987. Ben Bellitt, ed. and trans. *Residence on Earth & Other Poems.* New Directions Publishing Corporation, New York, 1973. Donald D. Walsh, trans.

O'Hara, Frank. *Selected Poems.* Random House, Inc., New York, 1974. Donald Allen, ed.

Ōtomo No Sakanoe, Lady. *100 Poems from the Japanese.* New Directions Publishing Corporation, New York, 1955. Kenneth Rexroth, trans.

Parker, Dorothy. *Poetry & Short Stories of Dorothy Parker.* Random House, Inc., New York, 1994.

Pastan, Linda. *An Early Afterlife. W. W. Norton & Company, Inc., New York, 1995.*

Paz, Octavio. *The Collected Poems, 1957–1987: Bilingual Edition.* New Directions Publishing Corporation, New York, 1987. Eliot Weinberger, ed. *Nostalgia for Death & Hieroglyph of Desire.* Copper Canyon Press, Port Townsend, Wash., 1993. Esther Allen & Eliot Weinberger, trans.

Plath, Sylvia. *The Collected Poems.* Harper Perennial, New York, 1992.

Rexroth, Kenneth. *Flower Wreath Hill: Later Poems.* New Directions Publishing Corp., New York, 1991.

Reznikoff, Charles. *Poems Nineteen Eighteen to Nineteen Seventy-Five: The Complete Poems of Charles Reznikoff.* Black Sparrow Press, Santa Rosa, 1989.

Rich, Adrienne. *Collected Early Poems 1950–1970.* W. W. Norton & Company, Inc., New York, 1993. *Dark Fields of the Republic: Poems 1991–1995.* W. W. Norton & Company, Inc., New York, 1995.

Rilke, Rainer Maria. *The Selected Poetry of Rainer Maria Rilke.* Vintage International Series, Random House, Inc., 1989. Stephen Mitchell, trans. *Translations from the Poetry of Rainer Maria Rilke.* W. W. Norton & Company, Inc., New York, 1938. M. D. Herter, trans.

Roethke, Theodore. *The Collected Poems of Theodore Roethke.* Doubleday & Co., Inc., New York, 1975.

Rukeyser, Muriel. *The Collected Poems of Muriel Rukeyser.* McGraw-Hill, Inc., New York, 1982.

Sandburg, Carl. *The Complete Poems of Carl Sandburg.* Harcourt Brace & Co., San Diego, 1970.

Sappho. *Sappho and the Greek Lyric Poets.* Schocken Books, Inc., New York, 1988. Willis Barnstone, trans.

Schwartz, Delmore. *Selected Poems*: *Summer Knowledge.* New Directions Publishing Corp., New York, 1967.

Sexton, Anne. *Complete Poems.* Houghton Mifflin Co., Boston, 1982.

Shakespeare, William. *A Choice of Shakespeare's Verse.* Faber & Faber, Inc., Winchester, 1971. Ted Hughes, ed.

Silverstein, Shel. *A Light in the Attic.* HarperCollins Children's Books, New York, 1981. *Where the Sidewalk Ends*: *Poems & Drawings.* HarperCollins Children's Books, New York, 1974.

Song, Cathy. *School Figures.* Poetry Series, University of Pittsburgh Press, Pittsburgh, 1994.

Sophocles. *The Three Theban Plays*: *Antigone*, *Oedipus*, *Oedipus at Colonus.* Viking Penguin, New York, 1982. Robert Fagles, trans.

Stafford, William. *The Darkness around Us Is Deep: Selected Poems of William Stafford.* HarperCollins, Inc., New York, 1993. Robert Bly, ed. *Learning to Live in the World*: *Earth Poems.* Harcourt Brace & Co., San Diego, 1994. Laura Apol, ed.

Stevens, Wallace. *The Collected Poems*. Random House, New York, 1990. *Opus Posthumous*. Random House, New York, 1990.

Swenson, May. *Nature: Poems Old & New*. Houghton Mifflin Co., Boston, 1994.

Szymborska, Wisława. *View with a Grain of Sand*. Harcourt Brace & Co., San Diego, 1995. Stainslaw Baranczak and Clare Cavanagh, trans. *Sounds, Feelings, Thoughts: Seventy Poems by Wisława Szymborska*. Princeton University Press, Princeton, N.J., 1981. Magnus J. Krynski and Robert A. Maguire, trans.

Thomas, Dylan. *Collected Poems*. New Directions Publishing Corp., New York, 1971.

Van Duyn, Mona. *If It Be Not I: Collected Poems*. Alfred A. Knopf, Inc., New York, 1992.

Walcott, Derek. *Collected Poems, Nineteen Forty-Eight to Nineteen Eighty-Four*. Farrar, Straus & Giroux, New York, 1987.

Whitman, Walt. *Complete Poetry & Selected Prose*. Houghton Mifflin Co., Boston, 1972. J. E. Miller, Jr., ed. *The Essential Whitman*. The Ecco Press, Hopewell, N.J., 1987. Galway Kinnell, ed.

Wilbur, Richard. *New & Collected Poems*. Harcourt Brace & Co., San Diego, 1989.

Williams, William Carlos. *The Collected Poems of William Carlos Williams, Vols. I and II*. New Directions Publishing Corp., New York, 1991. Walton Litz and Christopher McGawan, eds.

Wordsworth, William. *Poetical Works*. Oxford University Press, Inc., New York, 1973. Hellen Darbishire and Ernest De Selincourt, eds. *The Essential Wordsworth*. The Ecco Press, Hopewell, N.J., 1988. Seamus Heaney, ed.

Wylie, Elinor. *Collected Poems*. Alfred A. Knopf, Inc., New York, 1932.

Yeats, William Butler. *Collected Poems of W. B. Yeats*. Macmillan Publishing Co., Inc., New York, 1989.

About the Editors

Molly Peacock is the author of four books of poetry. Her most recent collection, *Original Love*, was published in 1995. President of the Poetry Society of America from 1989 to 1994, she divides her time between New York City and London, Ontario.

Elise Paschen is the Executive Director of the Poetry Society of America. Her first collection, *Infidelities*, won the Nicholas Roerich Poetry Prize for 1996, and is forthcoming from Story Line Press.

Neil Neches, Customer Services Manager for MTA New York City Transit, is a longtime enthusiast of poetry. He earned his MFA at Brooklyn College, and lives in Brooklyn.

Permissions

Anna Akhmatova, "Along the Hard Crest of the Snowdrift," translated by Jane Kenyon, from *From Room to Room* (Cambridge, Mass.: alicejames books, 1978). Copyright © 1978 by Jane Kenyon. Reprinted with the permission of Donald Hall.

Yehuda Amichai, "To My Love, Combing Her Hair," translated by Chana Bloch and Stephen Mitchell, from *The Selected Poetry of Yehuda Amichai*. English translation copyright © 1986 by Chana Bloch and Stephen Mitchell. Reprinted with the permission of HarperCollins Publishers, Inc.

A. R. Ammons, "Reflective from *The Really Short Poems of A. R. Ammons*. Copyright © 1990 by A. R. Ammons. Reprinted with the permission of W. W. Norton & Company, Inc.

Guillaume Apollinaire, "I Imagine Angels," translated by Kenneth Koch, from *Rose, Where Did You Get That Red?: Teaching Great Poetry to Childern* (New York: Random House, 1973). Copyright © 1973 by Kenneth Koch. Reprinted with the permission of the author.

W. H. Auden, "Lullaby" (excerpt) from *W. H. Auden: Collected Poems*, edited by Edward Mendelson. Copyright © 1976 by Edward Mendelson, William Meredith, and Monroe K. Spears. Reprinted with the permission of Random House, Inc.

Elizabeth Bishop, "Casabianca" from *The Complete Poems: 1927–1979*. Copyright © 1965 by Elizabeth Bishop. Copyright © 1979, 1983 by Alice Helen Methfessel. Reprinted with the permission of Farrar, Straus and Giroux, Inc.

Acknowledgments

Poetry in Motion would not have been possible without the inspiration, suggestions, and hard work of many.

We are particularly grateful to the following people at NYC Transit: Ivonne Barreras, Victor Chan, Margaret Coffey, Ira Lipton, Jack Lusk, Mary McCartney, Steve McClure, Barbara Orlando, Connie DePalma, Gabrielle Shubert, Barbara Spencer, Robin Stevens, and Darryl Tyree. Thanks also to Dan Allman, Erica Behrens, Laurie Callahan, Fred Courtright, Carol Flechner, Terence Kelly, Christian Red, Lisa Simmons, Florence Slade, Vera Stenhouse, P. A. Tippett, Matthew Waldman, Tim Walker, and John Wyatt.

We would also like to thank the Board of Governors of the Poetry Society of America—in particular John Barr, President, G. E. Murray, William Drenttel, Anna Rabinowitz, Mary Jo Salter, and Dana Gioia. Special thanks to the industrious staff of the PSA, especially Timothy Donnelly, Diana Burnham, and Susan Sully.

We are grateful to the Lila Wallace-Reader's Digest Fund, the National Endowment for the Arts, the New York State Council on the Arts, the New York City Department of Cultural Affairs, and the Chicago Community Trust for financial support of the PSA's programs. We would also like to thank the Opportunity Channel (Crosswalks Television Network Channel 72) for airing poems featured in Poetry in Motion.

Thanks, too, to those people who have helped to develop Poetry in Motion in

Chicago, in particular Constance L. Mortell and Annette Lee from the Chicago Transit Authority, Joseph Michael Essex and Nancy Denney Essex of Essex Two Incorporated, and the American Institute of Graphic Arts Chicago. We are also grateful to Jet Lithocolor Inc. and Potlatck Corporation, the City of Chicago Municipal Channels 23 and 49, and Richard M. Daley, Mayor, for airing selected poems on television.

Acknowledgment is due to those who inspired the inception of Poetry in Motion, including Milton Kessler, Joan Davidson, and the originators of London's Poems on the Underground: Judith Chernaik, Gerald Benson, and Cicely Herbert.

Finally, thanks to Elizabeth Anne Berney for her legal skills, Charles Verrill for his lessons in diplomacy, and Carol Houck Smith for recognizing the power of poetry.

Index of Poets and Translators